HEATHER PETERSEN

Adult ADHD & Autism

A few things I've learned~

Contents

Preface

I turn 45 this year. I am a mother of 2 beautiful boys born 18 years apart. My oldest son received his angel wings in 2014. I've been through marriage, divorce and several other relationships. I've experienced major traumas and abuses. I've blindly sat by as people I cared about took advantage of me. I was forced to leave a job I worked at for 12 years, in a field I've worked in my entire adult life.

I despise the word victim. I also really dislike drama. But, because I had no idea what ADHD was, let alone autism, especially for an adult woman, being a victim with a very dramatic life is what the outside world came to see me as. I fought against this tooth and nail. I know that I am different. I know somehow I just don't fit in. I also know that some things that are considered "normal" to other people, I struggle extremely hard with. Then there are things that are "normal" and easy for me that seem to baffle others. I've always wondered why humans make things so hard. "Humans" said in a way that implies I'm not human myself. I really feel like I am from some other place. Or more like I remember what life before this life was like. Boy have we complicated things!

My life has always been a game of copycat. I have learned to act and behave the way others close to me do. I also mimic characters in books or movies, even down to the way they talk and laugh. Prior to a year ago, I thought this is what all people did. I just assumed that this was how everyone learns. I was very confused as to why everyone else "got it" so well though. Because I still to this day feel like the odd man out. The awkward weirdo that never knows what to say next. I just stand there trying to pretend I know what's going on and end up tripping over all the words falling too quickly out of my mouth.

I am writing this very shortened story of mine to give hope to anyone else out there that may feel alone. I have felt alone my whole life. Even if there are people all around me, in relationships, etc., deep down inside, I feel alone. It sucks. I hope that my words will help you feel like you have at least one person in this world who understands how you feel. And, because ADHD can sometimes make reading LONG books kind of difficult, I condensed it to a little pocket book. So you can just carry me with you. :)

1

The Breakdown and Diagnosis

2020 was such a crazy year for the entire world. And not just that year itself, but it was the beginning of a whole different way of life for everyone. That was the year that covid happened. I had no idea what was in store for me. It wasn't even the actual illness of Covid 19 that would change my life. It was the way it changed life for all of us. In the first week of 2020, my very dearest soul friend passed from this life to the next. Looking back, I wonder if he knew what was about to transpire. He got out before the world went crazy!

In January and February of 2020 I remember first hearing about Covid. It never seemed like a big deal to me. I never could have anticipated that in March, the place I worked at for the last several years would tell my department, along with most others, that we would be working from home for the next 2 weeks. We were just going to flatten the curve right? I was frightened and shocked because this was something that was completely unheard of. I remember thinking that the world would never be able to recover after shutting down for 2 to 3 weeks! I often take things very literally. So when we weren't allowed to go back to the office at the end of 2 weeks, I fell apart. Fear took a strong hold on my life. I had been very specifically taught how to be a responsible adult. I followed that instruction precisely and didn't know any other way. The world would most certainly come to a complete stop if I couldn't continue my same 9 - 5, Monday through Friday job, like I'd done my whole adult life. How would I take care of my son and my family if I had to change the way I did things? I was pretty sure that if Covid didn't go away fast, it would mean the end of the world. I fought to get things back to "normal" as hard as I could. Being unable to accept change unfortunately caused me to fall. I fell hard.

Soon after I was sent home to work, I became my son's new 1st grade teacher too. I went from "knowing" how to be in this world to not having one single effing clue. I used to drop my child off at school where he had other adults to teach him math and reading. I would then have time to myself, driving in my car, listening to what I wanted, on my way to an office full of other adults. I had friends, co-workers, bosses, etc. who I interacted with. I went out to lunch. I had conversation, feedback, validation and the only social interaction I ever cared to have. Then, at the end of the day, I had more time to myself in my car, on the way to pick my son up from the babysitter. I had time to visit with him, ask how school went, laugh and chat amongst ourselves before arriving home. Once home, the routine was almost the same, every day. Dinner, clean up, get ready for bed..

All of the sudden I was thrown into a different life where all the characters had different parts. Now I was working from home. No need to get dressed up anymore. Could sleep in a little later. That was nice for a minute. Now I just headed to my desk to start working. I lost any alone time I once had while driving. All of my adult interactions were now over call or video, and they became very rare. I am not good at starting a conversation, let alone calling someone on purpose. I hate talking on the phone or making phone calls of any sort. I became a recluse. My friends and co-workers talked often, without me, because it was incredibly hard for me to talk electronically.

Now that I was also my son's teacher, usually I would need to get him started on school at the same time I was trying to work. I don't know how that was ever supposed to work. Most days, between working, teaching, making sure my son ate, keeping up on household chores, we were going until well after midnight every day!

I was in a constant state of confusion and fear. The way I had learned to be responsible and take care of my family, was no longer an option. I felt like I was drowning in a pool of unknown. I needed help. I needed direction. But everyone else in the world was just as confused as I.

By early 2021 I was starting to forget how to do my job. Things that I had known inside out with my eyes closed, I could no longer do. I started forgetting normal life things too. My partner would have conversations with me that I apparently participated in and would make decisions about. Three days later, when he would ask me about those things we'd discussed, I would look at him like he was crazy. I thought he was trying to start fights with me because I couldn't remember the things he was asking about. Slowly my brain just quit. I would be staring at my desk for 8 hours, completely unable to do any work. Right now, I cannot even explain what it was that was stopping me. I truly don't know. I just could not do my job no matter how hard I tried. I would sit and cry at my desk. My partner didn't understand and I would feel even worse when he would badger me about getting things done. This eventually led to me looking for a doctor and studying a lot of stuff online. I believed I had some sort of early onset dementia. There was no other explanation that made sense to me.

In June 2021 my dad came to live with me for his last week or so of this life. He had stage 4 lung cancer. My plan was to nurse him back to health so that he could go back home with his wife. It didn't turn out that way. That week he was with me, something in me took over. I wanted to take care of him. He trusted me and I loved having him in my home so that I could make sure he was ok. There wasn't anything I would rather do than care for my dad. I was miraculously able to handle all the phone calls, doctors appointments, giving medication, getting equipment delivered, getting home health nurses to the house regularly, getting him to eat and drink and back and forth to the restroom. I slept on the floor in his room so I could hear him. When he passed away I was devastated and shocked. I still handled the funeral and everything that needed to happen afterward. But when I tried to go back to work, I could not do it. I could not make my brain remember, as hard as I tried! In July 2021 I quit my job that I had been at for 12 years. It had been 23 years that I worked in accounting.

Right around that same time, I had just discovered I have ADHD. I began trying medications to see if they would help me. It wouldn't be until March of 2022 that I would learn that I am autistic as well. What I was experiencing was an autistic burnout. I still have not fully recovered.

2

Looking Back To Childhood

When I was being assessed for autism I learned that it is something that you have all your life. You don't just "get autism" at some point. If you are autistic, you always have been. How I was as a child was a big part of my assessment. I was amazed at all the signs and behaviors I had back then, and no one noticed. I guess it's probably because of timing. We are just barely coming to understand autism currently. Being the oldest child in my family, I don't think my parents had much to go off of. Neither did I. I just copied them and did what I was told.

I was always considered a nerdy kid in school. I was very shy and considered a goodie goodie. I had thick glasses and dressed in whatever I felt like. I HATED PE because I dreaded having to try and run, throw a ball, hit a ball, anything, while others watched me. I would get made fun of and laughed at. It was terrifying to me. A lot of times I would even try to stay inside during recess because I didn't have any desire to go "play" with other kids. I recall a time when I had walked over to the kindergarten playground at recess to see if I could see my little sister. I was so excited she was out there so I could just hang out with her! A teacher noticed and shooed me away telling me that I wasn't allowed to be over there. I think I cried. I was and am still, SO sensitive. I was academically very good in school when I was young. Thinking back, it's because I dreaded the idea of getting in trouble, making a mistake, being noticed for anything! I wanted to just get my school work done well so that I would stay off the teacher's radar.

Even though life seemed pretty boring and awful, it was actually different on the inside. I would always make up stories in my head and pretend that I was living them out. I would imagine that my favorite characters from movies were actually my friends, and would show up at school and save me from this life. Most of my life was lived in my imaginary made up worlds.

It wasn't until I was about 10 or 11 when I started feeling like I was really different from other kids. By this time I had made a few friends that I sometimes would hang out with. One of these friends would always tell me that she was trying to show me how to be a "cool kid" and not be a nerd anymore. She did this in a very kind way. She just thought that life would be hard for me if I was always being called a nerd. I remember her telling me how I needed to change my hair and fix the way I wore my clothes. My family didn't have a lot of money, so I wasn't able to shop for all the stylish expensive clothes. Thank God. I HATE shopping. And I couldn't care less about what clothes are in at the time. As long as I'm comfortable and they don't bug me, they do their job. But soon I realized that I had a lot more fun hanging out with my "nerd" friends. I had 2 of them that I spent a lot of time with. We could all be ourselves and talk about weird stuff, listen to our favorite music repeatedly, watch our favorite movies over and over, obsess about puberty and talk about what secret crushes we had. We could jump on the bed like little kids and be loud and messy and no one cared. But as junior high approached I felt I had to really start listening to my one friend, and change who I was completely. I wouldn't be able to survive being a shy, awkward, ugly, nerdy girl. On came the masks. I learned how to be whatever I needed to be for any situation. I watched my friends, I picked up attitudes and personas from characters in movies. I became so fake all the time. I was whoever I was with. Painfully, I grew apart from my 2 friends from elementary school. I followed my other friend in junior high and by the beginning of 9th grade I'd become close with my only other real friend throughout my whole childhood and young adult life. I ended up with 2 best friends who were on complete opposite sides of the pendulum. They hated each other and would fight over me all the time. One was part of the popular crowd and the other was part of the hippie alternative crowd. Ha ha ha! And I was very best friends with them both! Because I was who they told me to be.

I have to put in a little side note here. I obviously did not know I had ADHD or was autistic while I was growing up. I didn't know that what I was doing was different. I thought everyones' lives happened this way. I love both of these women to this day. Our relationships continued into adulthood. Nowadays, I mostly just see them on Facebook. We chat now and then but it breaks my heart that our younger kids don't even know each other. Because Facebook has made it possible to "kinda" stay in contact with people, I even get to see what my two best friends from elementary school are up to too! I am grateful to be able to see how people are doing, but I am a terrible friend. I don't know how to keep a friendship going. I don't know how or when or what to do to get together. I can't plan anything to save my life. I hate small talk or talking on the phone. I don't know what I am supposed to say if I even try to reach out. The reason I had these amazing friendships was because they did it. They cared about me. They took me in and taught me how to "be." They are the ones that kept them going as long as they did. I even remember them being upset with me for not doing my part. I didn't understand. I still don't. I try really hard. I wish I had a book of instructions on how to be a friend. Or be in any relationship for that matter. Tell me how often to call, how to plan an outing, what I should say in conversation. Tell me how close you get, whether I must hug them or not, what other kinds of affection people like. How often do I do all these things? Do I come on too strong, talk too much, laugh too loud? How do I know where to sit or stand if we are visiting in person? Do I look ok? How much do I tell them about my life? What if they want to go out? I really dislike being "out." I will do it for them though. If they even ever wish to speak to me after all this. I hope that if any of my friends ever read this, that they will know how much I love them and want to be part of their lives. I am sorry that I was a shitty friend. But now that I know a little more about my brain and why I am the way I am, maybe I can become a better friend and learn to cope with my weaknesses and use my strengths to be better in all that I do. Also! I am learning who *I* am! I probably have substance now! For most of my life I have been living behind my masks. So much so that I had no idea who Heather even was! Today, for the first time ever, I know who I am. For the last year I have been removing my masks. I still need them sometimes, but now I've had enough time to let myself peek through. It feels amazing! And guess what? I'm weird. I'm different. I'm awkward. And maybe that is ok.

3

Early Adulthood and On

Life wasn't easy for me. I always had to try so hard to just feel like I could fit in, in all areas of my life. I know that most kids follow their peers and tend to involve themselves in similar things as their friends. I tried doing that sometimes but I never felt like I belonged. I was so scared of everything, so afraid of looking like an idiot, that I never really had any activities or hobbies. I always had my imaginary life that I'd pretend was real inside my own head. I was never really good at making and keeping friends, so my imaginary life was full of much more adult ideas. I wanted so much to have one or two people who I knew would love and accept me no matter what. I wanted to be a mother, have a family, and have a partner. (I never realized at the time that my reasons for wanting a child so young were not healthy reasons to have a child ever. Nevertheless, I didn't know what I didn't know.) By the time I was a junior in high school I had made my imaginary story in my head, an actual thing in reality. I had a boyfriend who was one year older than me, and we decided to have a baby. On purpose. 16 and 17 years old. Sounds insane. It was. And I am SO grateful we did it. When I was 17 years old I gave birth to my first amazing little boy. Joey. His father and I were planning to get married and live happily ever after. That's how the stories in my head had always played out. Little did I know, well that's it. LITTLE did I know about anything. I had ZERO idea how to be a parent. I never even stopped to think about how I would feed and clothe and care for a baby. Did I even ponder that there would be a hospital bill? And that that was only the very beginning? Nope. I didn't. And fortunately my parents weren't the type that would kick me out on the streets. They, along with my partner's parents and family, took care of us all. In all the ways. At the very least, until we could take care of ourselves. I've probably never thanked them for that. If any of you are reading this, thank you. Truly, thank you. From the bottom of my heart.

Well, as you probably guessed, my happily ever after did not turn out. I didn't know how to have a relationship or a family any better than I knew how to be a friend. Mainly, I was still a child myself. But on top of all that, relationships of all types confused me. Humans baffle me. Honestly. I am as confused today about relationships as I was then! People make things so complicated. There are SO many unspoken rules. Assumptions are the norm. People talk with sarcasm, they "joke" around, they speak in riddles. Body language makes no sense. No one ever says what they actually mean and I am supposed to know what reading between the lines means?!? They talk with emotions and expect that everyone else will always know what they want and need at any given second. Or at least you better know... It's rude if you don't. It would be one thing if it was possible to learn how to read people, but everyone is different. Plus, no one wants and needs the same things all the time.

I have been in a lot of relationships. Different types, different people and different genders. I have never identified as straight. I don't feel like any certain label defines me either, and I've never quite understood why humans have such a need to have a certain title for each type of relationship. Obviously familial relationships are one thing. But as far as friendships and "romantic (for lack of a better word)" relationships go, there are far too many types to try and name them all. Plus, the connection between one person and another is **different** in EVERY case! Over time humans have created and enforced rules for relationships also. And different relationships have different rules. How the eff do you all understand all this? How do you define who gets more love, affection, time or attention? Who is more important? What types of affection are expected and/or allowed for each? Seriously? And why?? I truly believe that I remember life before here, and over there it is NOT this hard!

See, I love BIG. You wouldn't know it most of the time though. At least this is what I'm told. I apparently don't show affection in a way that most people realize it. I do work on this a lot, now that I understand. It hurts me to know that a lot of people that I really love/loved, never really thought I did. Emotions are confusing for me. I have them. I feel them. Sometimes I feel them very big. Sometimes I feel yours, mine and everyone else's. I am a very empathic person. I feel energy everywhere I am. My problem is the ability to put words to my feelings. And also how and when to express them. The way that I can think to explain it is there will be a huge cloud floating around me, consuming me. I can feel it. I know whether it is pleasant or not. I don't always know whether it is mine or someone else's, and I rarely can tell you what the actual feelings are until I've had some unknown amount of time to process through said cloud. It is extremely hard when I am being asked to talk about an issue or fight before I've had time to process. I've made SO many mistakes in this area, if you can even imagine. Angry partner needing answers right now. Ultimatums, etc. I will be thrown directly into meltdown mode, regardless of how hard I try not to. I will run away immediately if I can. If not, I will scream, cry, fall apart and say a whole bunch of stuff I don't mean. If I feel trapped and like I'm being attacked, I will melt down. No question. That certainly does not give me the right to be cruel, but what people don't understand is that I don't really have a choice. I will warn people, let them know that I need space to process my emotions. I tell them that I know what happens and the things that fall out of my mouth when they won't let me be. And if they continue to push me, I end up saying all sorts of mean things that I do not mean. I genuinely LOVE so much! I do not want to do this. Hopefully those reading this book will understand that sometimes there MUST be space. It's not that we are trying to escape. It is because we really love you! And we are trying to figure out what went wrong. Please let us show you this.

Before both of my diagnoses I believed that I was just a terrible person. I have had low self esteem my whole life. I couldn't understand how I could love so much and others didn't see it. I have tried EVERYTHING! To this day I am told that I am very cold and emotionless. That I don't have compassion or understanding for certain things. I will do things that I've learned others' like/need, but it is hard to continually keep doing an action that doesn't come natural to me. I forget. I still work on this, because I don't want to forget. I do care about other peoples' feelings. I want to show people I love them. I've been told so many times that loving me is hard. Having a relationship with me is hard. I've been told that I am selfish and I only care about myself. None of these things are true. I have spent my life trying to prove to people that these things are NOT true! And because of that, I have allowed people to hurt me, to walk on me, to abuse me, to use me... I became a people pleaser and never dared let my mask down. I wanted to be accepted. I wanted to have a family, especially having my sweet boy. So again, or still, I stayed fake. It is the ONLY way I knew how to survive. I started to believe that true love wasn't real. This life has just been too hard.

Since I was diagnosed with ASD in particular, things have started changing. As much as I dislike labels, for the first time in my life I know that I am not dumb. There are VERY VALID reasons for the way I am. My brain thinks and processes things differently than most of the world. We are all different of course. But now I understand why I've been so confused. This world and society wasn't built for brains like mine. And that is ok. I'm on a mission to create my own world. And I am not dumb.

I am smart. And no one gets to walk on me anymore. I will not let you.

4

Going Through Loss

My son Joey passed away suddenly in 2014. He was 19. He would be 27 now! I will not go into this too much because that is a whole other book. But that was the point where I fell down hard. And I never did get completely back up.

My youngest son was 9 months old when Joey passed away. My husband at the time was going through some legal issues that we were worried about. We were in the process of building a new home. I took 2 weeks off from work when Joey died, and because my boss went on maternity leave shortly after I returned and I was helping take over her responsibilities, I poured myself into work and acted like I was fine. I poured myself into my sweet baby. Being a mom was the only way I felt close enough to Joey. I kept my life and my mind as busy as possible so that I could survive the pain I felt inside. Eventually my marriage failed. I didn't even know how to wear my "wife" mask during that time. I wouldn't allow myself to be anything other than a good worker and a good mother. Everything else fell away. I was going to make sure that I could keep being responsible in the only way I knew how. I needed to be the best mother ever also, and I was going to try real hard to make it so my little guy would never experience pain. Fast forward a few years and

14

then a few more....

Everything broke. I started to forget how to do normal everyday things. I could not remember how to do my job. At least not very well. Life overwhelmed me because I could not put one foot in front of the other and move forward. My son who I had spoiled rotten was spoiled rotten. I only ever wanted to protect him and give him the world, but I'd held on to him so tightly, I waited on him hand and foot, that he thought that was normal. I had no idea what a disservice I was putting on him. And he struggled HARD when I started to change the rules. And I did too. I was so afraid to loosen my grip. I'd been through relationships back and forth that had and were still failing.... All this time that I thought I was supermom, super partner, super worker, super fake everything, I really wasn't any of it. I had this burning desire to be free. I was tired. I was so tired of listening to everyone else tell me how to do anything and everything in my life. It got too hard to pretend anymore. And when I broke, I broke hard.

This is all what led to me finding out about my ADHD and autism. And it should not have taken this much. I really should have given myself a damn break and known that I wasn't just stupid. I should have asked for help a long time ago. Please, if you, the person reading this now, has any suspicion about anything related to grief, autism, ADHD, depression, anxiety, mental health, ANY health, get help now. At least find a person you can trust and talk to them about it. Because no one should have to be that close to their death bed before getting any relief. Do you know what this kind of stress does to your physical body too? It is unreal. So please reach out. Talk to a friend. There are people out here that understand.

5

Let's Talk About It

We need to bring awareness to adult ADHD and autism. Especially in women. (But not exclusive to adults or female/male!) We need to talk about it and make it more common. There needs to be more resources out there so people don't feel so alone! We need a welcoming community of people of all sorts to talk about things that make us uncomfortable! How else are we ever going to bring about change? I almost checked out of this life because I was so lost and alone. It should not be that way. Let's do something about it.

6

Starting to Heal and Some Things I've Learned

ADHD and autism are thought to be mostly "kid" things. In fact, a lot of people still believe that autism is just something that young boys deal with. There is so much misinformation out there and we are just barely starting to understand things a little better. I am a 44 year old woman. I have been autistic all my life and I just found out less than a year ago! To me, finding out was life saving. I am just barely at the beginning of learning all there is to know. Even though I don't have much, I just wanted to point out a few things that I've learned.

Everyone has masks. I may have more than most. It's ok to use them when I need to and it's also really freeing to keep them off when I'm around safe people. I've learned who I really am this way. Ask yourself what it is that YOU actually want.

If a burnout happens and you lose certain functions, you must find a way to heal. You will probably gain them back again if so. But if you don't heal and love yourself, the chances are much smaller. I still am not where I once was in certain areas.

17

Some days are harder than others. My executive functions (time management, working memory, task initiation, self control, etc.) fluctuate. Be nice to yourself and just know that sometimes you just aren't going to get done what you wanted to. It's ok.

I am different. I like weird things. My special interest is coloring. I get mad if I can't color every day. I plan my days around coloring. So what? It is important to have time to do your special interest. It's also important though, to not forget that you also love other things too, like your children and family and stuff.

Get help from a professional about parenting. Because there are ways that you can make communication work with your family whether you are neurodivergent, neurotypical or anything else.

There is help out there. Not much. But there is help. Keep looking.

Some people care a lot about the way we say that we're autistic and/or how we talk about the levels. Person first language or vice versa and whether high functioning and low functioning labels are appropriate. I don't think my opinion is important here, and I want to be all inclusive, but it is important to look into.

Stimming is a must. I have changed which stims I've done over my life. Currently, I have lighters to spin and infinity cubes in all the rooms of my house. When I am stressed out, they calm me down a lot. They even make it possible to speak sometimes when I otherwise cannot.

I go into sensory overwhelm if I am not aware. Since my breakdown all of my senses are way too sensitive. Loud sounds hurt. I have noise canceling headphones and ear plugs that I use often. I can smell everything and sometimes it makes me sick. I really hate being touched unless I am expecting it and am ok with it.

Now I know why sexuality has always been a weird thing for me. I honestly don't get the point really, unless you want to have kids. But I haven't met one person that agrees with me, so it's a challenge I'm still working on.

I've heard that it's common for autistic women to have gut issues. I do and I've had them all my life.

Now I know why I am late ALL THE TIME. I am time blind. I still try to fix it and some days are better than others.

I get obsessed with some things so much that I don't want to do anything else ever. It makes my family mad and I'm constantly working on it. Right now it's coloring and art.

I take things very literally. Sarcasm is hard for me to understand. I am very gullible and it's gotten me in trouble. I have to constantly be careful with this.

I have to remember that I deal with emotions and feelings different than most people around me. I see relationships differently and most things really. I try to remember that I am not always "right" but I am not always wrong either. Just because I see things differently does not mean that I am wrong or invalid. It also doesn't mean that others will agree with me. It takes a lot of work and communication to come to agreements with others on some things. I've had to accept that certain things just are what they are. But I will not stop trying to bring awareness, change, communication and community to these things!

Some people don't believe me. Some people are mean. So I just don't go around those people anymore than I must.

I LOVE BIG. I have the most genuine heart. I am learning how to better let others know that I love them. I'm learning to be less harsh with my words and actions.

I am not a social person. I love to talk to people without having to be around them.

Some people care about whether others self diagnose. There are a lot of reasons why one would choose to get a diagnosis or not. I personally have no room to judge one way or the other. I love you just the same. I happened to get diagnosed as it was possible for me to do so.

I didn't know that there were so many different ways to better use my strengths and learn to deal with my weaknesses. I am still learning. It's possible to make life easier than it was before.

7

Conclusion

Thank you~ If this book has helped or interested you, I would be so grateful if you would leave a review on Amazon. Namaste~